MW00861713

LEGAL DUTIES

FOR DIRECTORS

An Association Board Member's Guide to
Avoiding Risk While Advancing the Mission

JERALD A. JACOBS

asae
association
management
press

WASHINGTON, DC

The author has worked diligently to ensure that all information in this book is accurate as of the time of publication and consistent with standards of good practice in the general management community. As research and practice advance, however, standards may change. For this reason it is recommended that readers evaluate the applicability of any recommendations in light of particular situations and changing standards.

ASAE: The Center for Association Leadership
1575 I Street, NW
Washington, DC 20005-1103
Phone: (202) 626-2723; (888) 950-2723 outside metropolitan Washington, DC area
Fax: (202) 220-6439
Email: books@asaecenter.org

We connect great ideas and great people to inspire leadership and achievement in the association community.

Keith C. Skillman, CAE, Vice President, Publications, ASAE: The Center for Association Leadership

Baron Williams, CAE, Director of Book Publishing, ASAE: The Center for Association Leadership

Cover by Beth Lower, Art Director, ASAE: The Center for Association Leadership
Interior design by Troy Scott Parker, Cimarron Design

This book is available at a special discount when ordered in bulk quantities. For information, contact the ASAE Member Service Center at (202) 371-0940. A complete catalog of titles is available on the ASAE website at www.asaecenter.org.

ISBN-13: 978-0-88034-373-2
ISBN-10: 0-88034-373-7

Printed in the United States of America.

10 9 8 7 6 5 4 3 2 1

CONTENTS

PREFACE

So you've been elected to the board of directors of your association. Congratulations! It promises to be an exhilarating experience, what with combined opportunities to advance and improve the association and the services it provides for members, to network with colleagues whom you respect but may not know well yet, and to enjoy a bit of professional prestige and resume enhancement that the board position inevitably affords. Who knows? This might be the first step toward becoming an officer of the association, and maybe even someday assuming the chief elected officer position. Perchance to dream....

Before getting too carried away with the career victory that your board seat represents, there is a big cooler of icy Gatorade on the sidelines waiting to be dumped over you. Besides being a tribute and reward for the respect that you've earned in your field, there are also serious responsibilities that come with the job of association director. Who knew? In fact, there is an overwhelming body of established law which states that board members of nonprofit organizations such as your association, even though most board members serve as volunteers and without compensation, automatically assume individual legal obligations and personal legal risks by serving in their positions. No worries, as they say Down Under; this is certainly not a reason to reconsider accepting the position. What you will need to understand, and be careful about, is always based on simple common sense and familiar concepts of right and wrong. There are some quirks. They're easily grasped. The whole purpose of this guide is to help you do that quickly and painlessly.

You're not the first person to face this situation. Associations and association directors have been around as long as our country has. In his published notes from traveling throughout the newly independent United States of America in the early 1800s, the French commentator Alexis de Toqueville repeatedly observed that there were already thousands of volunteer organizations throughout the land. He said that when a new endeavor would be undertaken by the government in France, or by a man of rank in England, you can be sure that it would be undertaken instead by an association or society in the United States. Tax exemption statistics suggest that there are currently at least 60,000 trade associations, professional societies, or other membership organizations in this country, which together we're calling *associations* here. All of them have governing boards; and all of them have board members.

This guide attempts to summarize for volunteer association directors, like you, the major areas of legal risk—both for those kinds of organizations and for the directors themselves. There is a chapter addressing each of the major areas of legal or compliance risks for directors. These chapters provide context for the deliberations and decisions that association directors typically face. And, to help demonstrate the risks, each of those chapters includes real-life stories drawn from actual cases or controversies (but with true identities disguised). As the famous Santayana quote states, "those who cannot learn from the past are doomed to repeat it."

This guide is no more than a summary; many texts have been published on the legal aspects of associations. A subjective list is included in the "Resources" section of this book. The serious student of association law is referred there. This guide does not aim to provide a comprehensive overview of all laws applicable to associations, but instead is focused on your personal obligations as a director.

So, congratulations again on the honor of your association board position. And chill out. Once you get a feel for what's expected of you as an association director from a legal and compliance point of view, you'll perform like a champ!

The author is deeply grateful to several colleagues/friends who helped prepare this guide: Dawn Crowell, Alvin Dunn, Emily Erlingsson, Patrick Jennings, Julia Judish, and Fred Lowell; nevertheless any inadequacies of the guide are the author's alone.

   – Jerry Jacobs
     Washington, DC
     June 2014

What Is an Association?

B
EFORE YOU CAN EFFECTIVELY serve in a governance role for your association, you ought to understand the main characteristics of associations. Each one has a bearing on your responsibilities. So here goes. An association usually has four characteristics that together make it different from other kinds of entities. It is (1) a nonprofit corporation, and (2) a tax-exempt organization, that is (3) governed by volunteer leaders, often on behalf of (4) voting/dues-paying members. Each feature has important legal ramifications, which provide the foundation for everything else discussed in this guide.

Nonprofit Corporation

A *nonprofit corporation* is a corporation that is officially chartered under the laws of a state government. Ordinarily the criteria that must be met as conditions of obtaining a state charter include a prohibition against the nonprofit corporation issuing equity stock and a requirement that it be governed according to the chartering state's laws for nonprofit corporations. The "nonprofit" characterization is a bit misleading; there is no prohibition against the corporation in one or more years having an excess of revenues over expenditures (typically called "surplus," not "profit," in the nonprofit field). The point, though, is that a nonprofit corporation—as distinguished from a for-profit corporation—exists first and foremost for reasons other than making money for shareholders. It may be to advance a business area, a profession, or a cause; it may be to pursue charitable, scientific, or religious goals. But it does not have equity owners; indeed nonprofit corporations are technically not owned by anyone (some refer to them as "quasi-public"). In addition, to become and to remain a nonprofit corporation, the entity must be governed according to the state's nonprofit corporation laws, which exist in every state. These laws spell out the rights and obligations of the entity itself, as well as of its leadership and its members.

In some states the charter document may be called *articles of incorporation* or a *certificate of incorporation;* and nonprofit corporations may be called *not-for-profit, non-stock, non-equity,* or *mutual benefit* corporations in some states. Those distinctions in denominations have no practical differences. U.S. nonprofit corporations are all pretty much the same no matter what state is chosen as the state of incorporation and no matter what that state calls its nonprofits.

Tax-Exempt Organization

A *tax exempt organization* is a nonprofit corporation that has been determined by the Internal Revenue Service (IRS) to be exempt from paying federal income taxes on any net of revenues over expenditures—its surplus—each year. This is a wonderful advantage, of course, since for-profit business corporations must pay income taxes on their net returns, currently at rates up to 35 percent. The most fundamental requirements for tax exemption are: (1) that the organization is formed as a nonprofit; and (2) that the organization does not allow its assets to provide advantages to individuals (*inure* is the uncommon term used in the law). In order to be determined by the IRS to be tax-exempt, organizations submit a comprehensive application which is subject to a lengthy review. There are numerous categories of federal tax exemption; the one that often best fits trade associations, professional societies, and other membership organizations is Section 501(c)(6) of the Internal Revenue Code.

Other organizations that enjoy federal tax exemption in other categories may resemble Section 501(c)(6) organizations— scientific or educational membership organizations under Section 501(c)(3), cause and social welfare membership organizations under Section 501(c)(4), or agricultural membership organizations under Section 501(c)(5) (which is also the category that applies to unions). The principles discussed here are usually equally applicable to those other kinds of exempt organizations; but they may have additional considerations as well. For example, those with Section 501(c)(3) or 501(c)(4) exemption have a particular prohibition against providing excess benefits to certain volunteers or staff (i.e., paying anything to them at more than market rates). This reflects, but is more specific than, the prohibition against inurement applicable to all exempt organizations.

Income received by a tax-exempt association from programs and activities related to the purposes for which the association received exemption are not subject to federal income tax. But net income from other programs or activities unrelated to the purposes for which the association originally received exemption is indeed subject to tax (called *unrelated business income tax (UBIT)*). An exempt association can have modest amounts of UBIT year after year with no untoward consequences. But if unrelated income becomes substantial compared to exemption-related income, the association's whole income tax exemption status is in jeopardy.

Many states have their own income tax laws; usually they also have tax-exemption schemes similar to the federal one.

Governance

An organization *governed by volunteers* means that the principal decision-making mechanism of an association is the governing board. The board consists of individual directors who are drawn from the field represented by the association and who serve voluntarily without compensation (although expenses are sometimes reimbursed). Typically the board elects officers who often form an executive committee to govern during the periods between board meetings. Although volunteer board members usually serve without compensation, that does not mean that that they are also without legal responsibilities. In fact serious personal and individual liability can be imposed upon association board members who fail to live up to those responsibilities. Depending upon its size and budget, the association may also maintain employed executive staff who report to the board. The volunteer governance of an association means that decision making sometimes occurs more slowly than in a business corporation and transactions can be more cumbersome. The fact that the board composition churns regularly raises singular challenges when attempting to maintain consistent long-term policies and programs. Finally volunteer board members of associations tend to be more risk-averse than board members of for-profit business entities.

Membership

Many associations have *voting* and/or *dues-paying members* but not all of them. There are organizations we call associations that either do not have members at all, or do not have members with a right to vote or an obligation to pay dues; everything else discussed here applies to those kinds of associations as well. Where the association has members, and where its governing documents (the charter or the bylaws) provide voting rights for the members, typically it is those members who elect the governing board; members may also have the right to vote to approve changes to the bylaws. State law also dictates other features pertaining to voting members, such as annual membership meetings or the rights of members to access association information. Associations with members commonly require those members to pay dues as a condition of maintaining membership; there may be various dues categories at different payment levels and with different membership prerogatives. Courts have characterized the governing documents of an association, particularly the bylaws, as effectively an agreement between the organization and its members specifying the rights and obligations of the entity and of the members. Thus bylaws are not to be treated casually or inconsistently.

What Makes an Organization an Association?[1]

Nonprofit corporation	A state charter declaring the organization to be a corporation that exists for reasons other than profit-making for shareholders
Tax-exempt organization	Determined by the Internal Revenue Service to be exempt from federal income tax because it is a nonprofit and does not use assets to provide advantages to individuals
Governance	Elected or appointed directors who serve without compensation but nonetheless have serious legal responsibilities to the association
Members who vote and pay dues (not in all associations)	Individuals or firms that meet membership criteria and join to receive member benefits and voting rights in return for paying specified dues

---

[1] These characteristics generally apply to associations.

Your Responsibilities as a Board Member

BOARD MEMBERS OF ASSOCIATIONS are usually called *directors* but also sometimes *trustees* among other titles. Even though they serve voluntarily and without compensation, association directors have fiduciary duties—including duties of both care and loyalty—to their associations. What that means for you is that you must remain loyal to the association and its cause; that means, in essence, that you are required to act reasonably and in the best interests of the association. In the event that an element of these duties is disregarded and violated, you would be breaching your duty and could be held personally and individually liable to the association or to others for whatever damages are caused. Your duty as an association director, and the resulting risk to you, is not theoretical or academic. There are actual reported cases in which directors of nonprofit organizations have been held financially responsible for neglecting their duties.

There is one central legal principle—and three corollary ones—encompassed in the concept of a board member's fiduciary duty.

The Duty of Loyalty and Care

This duty is very broad, and frankly, a bit subjective. While in your role as an association director, you must put the association's interests ahead of your own interests. Think of a parent's relationship with a son or daughter; most parents will put their child's needs and interests first. That's the essence of what is required of you as a board member—looking out for the well-being of the association and not, first and foremost, for your own well-being. In the language typically used in court pronouncements on this principle, a director is required to exercise ordinary and reasonable care in the performance of the director's duties, exhibiting honesty and good faith. The principle is admittedly somewhat vague; but it is applied in particular fact situations in which a director's decisions are questionable as to whether they were made for the association or director's own interests. Courts have said that an association board member has the obligation to exercise care and caution when acting on behalf of the association, to attempt to avoid generating legal liability for the association, and to attempt to further the association's collective interests rather than the board member's own interests or the interests of any other parties. The duty might seem more concrete once you understand its three corollaries.

The Duty to Avoid Conflicts of Interest

The general duty of loyalty and care encompasses a more specific duty to avoid conflicts of interest in order to assist the association in maintaining bias-free decision making in governance. Even talking about conflicts among association volunteers is awkward. There is often a suggestion of wrongdoing, disloyalty, or cheating. In fact that climate need not pervade conflicts management. Basically a conflict may exist when a volunteer director partic-ipates in the deliberation and resolution of an issue important to the association while the director, at the same time, has other professional, business, volunteer, or family responsibilities outside of the association that could predispose or bias the director one way or another regarding the issue before the association. The problem has more to do with the appearance of bias than with out-and-out adversity or even dishonesty. The association and its constituency have a right to unbiased governance. So the board of directors of the association is responsible for defining what the association considers to be a conflict and for determining when a director may have an unacceptable conflict.

The best way to drain the emotion from conflicts issues is to have a policy already in place and a process that is routine and automatic. Some states, in fact, require these for nonprofits. Directors are required to declare their potential conflicts—their other interests—and then the rest of the association's leadership takes over and decides what, if anything, to do about those conflicts. The leadership might regard the mere disclosure of a director's conflicts to be a sufficient cure. The rest of the directors are made aware of the disclosing director's other interests and are advised to take them into account when that director debates and decides related issues that come before the board. The vast majority of conflicts situations are resolved just through disclosure. The leadership might decide that, in fact, the conflicts that a director has disclosed are serious and pervasive, with a different reaction warranted to demonstrate the absence of bias in the association's decision making. The director might be asked to refrain (recuse) from participating in board deliberation or decisions on the matter. In extreme cases of pervasive conflicts the director might even be asked to resign as a director.

It is common for the director who has another interest that meets the association's definition of conflicts to declare that the director is comfortable acting in the association's best interests. The director then expects the conflicts issue to immediately be dropped from consideration by the association. But the law is clear that it is principally the association's prerogative, not that of the director, to manage conflicts. The association can most efficiently do so by adopting, through its board, a clear definition of conflicts, requiring disclosure by directors, and then dispassionately determining what to do in each instance of disclosure.

The Duty to Maintain Confidentiality

Another director's obligation encompassed by the duty of care is maintaining confidentiality. While it seems self-evident, in fact nonprofit organization directors often somehow do not ascribe the same importance to confidentiality of association information as they do to the importance of confidentiality in their own businesses or professions. There are many issues that arise for an association board of directors that require confidentiality in the best interests of the association. Reports on negotiations for real estate transactions; discussions of litigation or legislative strategy; information about personnel matters; decisions on interpretation of standards, issuance of certification, or enforcement of ethics are but a few examples. In general, information about board deliberations—as opposed to board decisions that are summarized in meeting minutes—are considered confidential in order to protect directors' ability to discuss views freely and frankly at board meetings. You should be alert to any information that comes your way in your board member capacity where the confidentiality of that information obviously has value to the association or, in the converse, where disclosure could pose risks or injury to the association. But you should also be careful to avoid disclosure of any information that might be regarded as confidential and check with the CEO or board chairman before presuming that such information is available to be disclosed.

The Duty to Respect Corporate Opportunities

A final duty of loyalty and care corollary, one that perhaps manifests less frequently than conflicts and confidentiality, involves competing with the association. As a director you are specifically prohibited from engaging in competition with the association itself for business or professional prospects. Directors may generally engage in the same line of business or areas of endeavor as the association, provided it is done in good faith and without injury to the association. But one form of competition that is not permitted is appropriating *corporate opportunities.* A corporate opportunity is a business prospect, idea, or investment that is related to the activities or programs of the association and that the director knows, or should know, would be in the best interests of the association to accept or pursue. You may take advantage of such a corporate opportunity independently of the association only after it has both been offered to, and rejected by, the association, as well as after full disclosure to the association of your pursuit of the opportunity.

Beyond the duty of loyalty and care for association directors and its corollaries, there are several strong influences that compel you as a director to be concerned about good governance.

Apparent Authority

An aspect of the directors' duties to the association—not specifically related to fiduciary or loyalty duty—is that of apparent authority. The U.S. Supreme Court has held that illegal activities of someone acting on behalf of an association are the legal responsibility of the association if the person only just appeared to be acting with the authority of the association—even when the association's board of directors did not approve the activities, did not benefit from them, and did not even know about them. This means that associations, lest they become legally liable for anything volunteers do or say that even appears to be done or said with the associations' permission, must be careful to limit who is authorized to act or speak for the associations. Directors in particular, whom one would ordinarily expect to be representing the association officially by virtue of their board positions, should never assume they have the power to represent their association unless they are given specific authorization to do so. In short, check first before proceeding to make pronouncements or take actions in what you think are the best interests of the association.

Sarbanes-Oxley Law of 2002

The standards of appropriate conduct for directors of associations are evolving rapidly, owing in part to the legislative governance reforms for publicly traded business corporations under the Sarbanes-Oxley Law of 2002. There are two features of Sarbanes that apply to all entities, including associations, and carry criminal penalties for violations: (1) the provisions prohibiting destruction of documents in connection with federal investigations, and (2) the provisions prohibiting retaliation against whistle-blowers who report federal violations. But other corporate governance principles of Sarbanes, while not strictly applicable to associations, have been largely adapted in the association community. They include: (a) a governing board that defines its own central role in setting policy and providing oversight, (b) the independence of the board from management, (c) an audit committee with authority over auditors and audits, (d) a code of conduct for governance, (e) a plan for overseeing CEO compensation, and (f) complete and accurate financial disclosure. Increasingly you and the association's whole board will be expected to adopt these now-universal best practices for governance.

IRS Form 990

More recently, the Internal Revenue Service (IRS), at the instigation of the U.S. Congress, decided to advance good governance for tax-exempt organizations by including governance disclosures in the annual tax return that these organizations, including associations, must file. That return is the Form 990 that was first required for the 2009 tax year. There are more than a dozen governance issues raised in the Form 990; the most important ones are: (1) conflicts of interest, (2) whistle-blower protection, (3) document retention and destruction, (4) determining compensation, and (5) joint ventures with for-profit businesses. In asking that organizations annually disclose their practices in these areas, the IRS is clearly attempting to require, not just suggest, that they adopt what IRS believes are best governance practices. There are risks, at least to you and your association's reputation, in failing to do so.

STORIES FROM LIFE

"Director-as-Defendant"

How can violation of your duty of care as an association director get you in trouble? Easy. Here's what happened to some other association directors.

A state-wide trade association thrives on its major annual trade show, which provides the largest portion of the association's revenues. Jim and Jane are elected to the association's board of directors. They are thrilled to accept the recognition and prestige of sitting on the governing board of their state association. Jim and Jane happen to be overwhelmingly preoccupied with their own growing businesses. Both find that they just cannot lend their valuable time to the association's board activities. Neither manages to attend board meetings and both largely ignore periodic reports that they receive as directors. During their terms on the board, the trade association is rocked by a major crisis. In the face of competition from a commercially owned show, the association's trade show quickly shrinks in size and then fails completely. The annual show must be cancelled. The financial impact is so serious that the association becomes insolvent. The association's major creditors, including its headquarters office landlord and the convention centers where its trade shows had been scheduled for future years, exhaust their claims against the association itself. The creditors turn next to sue Jim and Jane, alleging that they are personally liable for the association's debts because they failed to give even minimal attention to their duties as directors. After a lengthy court proceeding, Jim and Jane are found personally liable for a share of the debts of the now-defunct association.

"Opportunities Knocking"

If application of the corporate opportunities doctrine to association directors seems remote, consider this situation.

A national professional society in a rapidly expanding technology field maintains a distinguished governing board of highly respected professionals in that field. The Chairman of the Board is approached by representatives of a start-up business corporation to provide the names of some prominent professionals in the society who would be willing to sit on the corporation's fledgling expert advisory council along with others. The start-up corporation wants to use its relationship with these professionals to show lenders and customers both gravitas and credibility based on the reputations of the professionals. The society's chairman considers the matter and ultimately decides to provide the names of the society's officers—its whole executive committee—to serve on the advisory council of the start-up. Each of the officers is given corporate stock in gratitude for this service. Eventually the start-up becomes wildly successful. Years later each of the professional society's now-former officers realizes seven figures in stock appreciation. The society's current leadership learns of this result and brings a claim against the former officers based on the corporate opportunities doctrine. The former officers settle by turning over much of their stock appreciation to the association.

What Are Your Main Legal Duties as a Board Member?

Loyalty and care	You have an obligation to be attentive and conscientious about the organization, its well-being, its policies and programs, and its governance
Conflicts of interest	You must disclose situations in which you might have other interests adverse to those of the association or that compete with the association's interests; then you must resolve the conflicts as directed by the association
Confidentiality	You must maintain the confidentiality of whatever information the association needs to keep confidential to advance the best interests of the association
Corporate opportunities	You must not take advantage of any business or financial opportunity that emerges from your service to the association as a director, at least not without the association's approval

Risks from Antitrust

O NE OF THE MOST serious kinds of legal challenges that any association can face is an antitrust challenge. As an association director, you should be alert for antitrust risks almost instinctively. The law books are rife with reports of antitrust judgments against associations, and in a few cases against association directors, going back a century. Defending and resolving an antitrust case often takes years and costs a fortune, not to mention the adverse publicity and diversion from mission while the case is pending. The most acute risk is to trade associations, because the antitrust laws exist to regulate business conduct. But beginning fifty years ago cases have been brought against professional societies as well. Associations formed to advance causes, science, education, or philanthropy have the lowest antitrust risk. Here's a summary of the policies and programs of associations that can lead to potential antitrust exposure.

Antitrust Generally

The federal antitrust laws are intended to promote open and fair competition in all commercial endeavors. Most fundamentally they mandate that businesses and professionals must make important business decisions—for example, setting prices or deciding with whom to do business—independently and not in concert with competitors. State antitrust laws have the same objectives.

Associations are voluntary organizations of members, many of which compete with one another. Virtually any action that an association takes toward private regulation of an industry or profession may raise antitrust issues. Many of these actions are perfectly lawful, such as standard setting, certification of products or professionals, and dispute resolution. You need to take great care, however, to ensure that your association's self-regulation activities do not fall within the special unlawful categories established by the courts as *anticompetitive.* The courts consider an action to be anticompetitive when, on balance, it raises prices or fees or limits the quantity or quality of available goods or services. Prices and fees, in fact, are a particularly sensitive area. Even action that may only indirectly affect prices and fees, such as association-promulgated arrangements on terms and condition of sale, warranties, limitations on the extent or type of advertising, and hours of operation, can also be expected to attract antitrust scrutiny.

Violations of the antitrust laws may be prosecuted by the federal government, either civilly or criminally, and by private persons or firms alleging antitrust injury. Courts may award injunctive relief against violators and may require violators to pay victims three times the financial injury actually suffered (called *treble damages*), plus their attorneys' fees.

Discussions at Meetings

Meetings may be the most universally common activity of associations. It is through meetings, first and foremost, that associations fulfill their essential mission of assisting members in communicating to one another, networking with one another, and learning from one another. Association meetings are also necessary to carry out the governance functions of associations.

It is important to note that association meetings also present unique opportunities for violations of the law to occur. Antitrust conspiracies can be, and often have been, developed through discussions at association meetings. Defamation can occur, infringement liability can be incurred, and other legal risks are present. It is obvious that associations are not always in control, and therefore cannot always police, the discussions at association meetings. Your association should be careful to ensure that, at least when you are in charge of what is discussed at association meetings, there is due regard paid to the legal ramifications of those discussions.

In the antitrust context, courts have often stretched to find that attendees at meetings have agreed upon joint anticompetitive business conduct. It is certainly not necessary, when government or private challengers are attempting to prove an antitrust conspiracy, to show that the alleged conspirators actually signed a document committing themselves to illegal conduct, or even to show that they agreed clearly in conversations to commit to the conduct. Discussions at meetings in which the plans for a conspiracy were signaled among the meeting attendees, followed by parallel anticompetitive activity of the attendees consistent with the discussions, have been sufficient to support an antitrust violation.

Thus, in inviting speakers, preparing agendas and minutes, and monitoring discussions at association meetings, the maximum control possible should be exercised to avoid suggestions of antitrust impropriety.

Membership Decisions

Membership in an association is ordinarily available in one or more categories to entities or individuals meeting criteria set out in the bylaws. Associations that deny applications for membership, or terminate existing members, run a risk of legal challenge unless the reasons for denial or termination are clear, reasonable, and straightforward ones—for example, nonpayment of dues, failure to meet objective definitions of eligibility, or unwillingness to comply with a reasonable code of ethics. In fact, many associations have been required to defend against legal challenges resulting from adverse membership eligibility decisions. In general, the more important membership in an association is for employment, engagement, sales, work assignment, or reimbursement in a business, profession, or field, the more closely a court will scrutinize membership criteria and procedures and the more readily the court will overturn what it perceives to be unreasonable criteria or unfair procedures. Associations are not social clubs; membership decisions may well come under legal attack if they even seem to be made based on anything other than whether the applicant meets the published criteria.

Antitrust laws have often been applied to invalidate denial or termination of association membership. Where a challenger can show that association membership has significant competitive value, and was withheld by the association on arbitrary or unreasonable grounds, the finding of an antitrust violation is likely.

Separately or together with the theory of antitrust liability, the denial or termination of association membership can also be overturned on the theory of fairness—failure of the association to afford fundamental due process. In most states, basic due process requirements apply to association membership decisions and mandate at least: (1) notice of the basis of the decision to the person whose membership is to be denied or terminated, and (2) opportunity to respond to the association's notice.

Price or Fee Data

Many associations have as one of their central activities the collection and dissemination of information about prices, costs, credit risks, production or sales levels, or other statistics about the businesses, professions, or fields represented by the associations. Surveys to collect this data can be undertaken with little legal risk unless the information exchanged becomes the basis for anticompetitive agreements among the recipients of the information.

Association surveys must not be used to facilitate illegal agreements among members to fix prices or fees; establish uniform production or service levels; allocate markets or customers; or boycott suppliers, competitors, clients, or customers. There is also the risk that dissemination of inaccurate data could involve defamation.

Steps should be taken to minimize the ability of members to use association-published statistical information for illegal ends: (1) only gross sales, or average prices or fees, or other composites should be reported; (2) no composite data should be reported in a category where only a few submissions were received; (3) individual submissions should be accorded confidentiality; (4) only past information, not projected future prices or fees, should be reported; (5) participation in any statistical program should be voluntary; and (6) the association should not make exhortations or recommendations for action by members based on the information.

Codes of Ethics

Many associations promulgate and enforce codes of ethics for their memberships. These codes set forth both desirable goals and behavioral requirements considered essential for the protection of the public and for the optimal development of the association's field. Enforcement ordinarily occurs according to a detailed set of procedures intended to ensure objectivity and fairness. Both the establishment of ethical requirements and their enforcement are legally sensitive areas.

Some code of ethics provisions are especially suspect; examples include provisions that: (1) set or suggest maximum or minimum prices or fees; (2) limit or discourage nondeceptive advertising; and (3) suggest boycotts of suppliers, competitors, or customers/patients/clients. But many ethical rules of associations are pro-competitive—they result in better products or services, increased availability or access, or lower prices or fees. All ethical rules must be evaluated to ensure that the motives and effects enhance competition and not reduce it. In any challenge the issue will usually be whether the code provisions were considered reasonable.

It is equally important that association codes of ethics be promulgated and enforced using adequate procedures. Associations can impose discipline, of course, only upon their members. In doing so, the law requires that associations be careful to use procedures to assure due process. Minimal due process includes: (1) written notice outlining the alleged violation, possible sanctions, and right to respond; (2) unbiased review of all charges and evidence from both the complaining party and the responding party; and (3) the right to appeal an adverse decision to an unbiased separate decision-making body.

Standards, Testing, and Certification

Since colonial times, associations have issued statements on common terminology, simplification of parts or styles, and uniform design or performance specifications. Tens of thousands of association-promulgated standards are now in place. Associations that have developed standards have often taken the next steps and engaged in testing and certification of products or services against the established standards. These endeavors have manifest benefits: They raise the level of competition, provide common targets and goals, simplify ordering and communication, help assure interchangeability of parts, and provide assurance to the public that products and services with association certification meet standards of high quality. Programs of privately issued standards, testing, and product/service certification are always voluntary—there is no compulsion of law for compliance or participation; nevertheless, government agencies have often adopted association product programs or service quality programs through mandatory regulations.

The basic legality of association-sponsored standards, testing, and product/service certification programs has frequently been affirmed by courts. But legal challenges have also resulted in adverse rulings, from which some general guidelines can be distilled: (1) the programs must not be used as vehicles for raising, lowering, or stabilizing prices or fees; (2) they must not result in excluding competitors; (3) they must not limit production or availability; (4) performance standards are preferable to design standards; (5) standards should reflect state-of-the-art technology; (6) the programs must be voluntary; (7) even nonmembers should have access to the programs; and (8) interpretation of standards, testing, or certification requirements should be nonbiased.

Professional Certification

Associations of individual professional members, whether of traditional licensed professionals or others, very often operate or sponsor professional certification programs. The association will promulgate a list of educational, experience, or testing criteria as the basis for its certification; and then the association will assess candidates' qualifications against the criteria, often including a certification examination. Established association professional certification can often be a crucial, or even essential, credential for professional employment or engagement, reimbursement for services, or advancement in the field.

Antitrust-based challenges have often been leveled against professional certification programs when those denied a credential have maintained that the criteria were unreasonable or assessments were unfair. Two elements are key to avoiding antitrust or other legal problems in this area. First, certification criteria should be valid and appropriate—reasonable—as the basis for measuring the professional competence of candidates. Any element of economic or competitive motive in establishing the criteria runs risks. Second, and equally important, there must be complete fairness— due process—in evaluating applications, administering exams, and scoring decisions. This means unbiased individuals must accord fair procedures to all candidates equally.

STORIES FROM LIFE

"To Advertise or Not To Advertise"

How do you as an association director make sure that antitrust risks are avoided? Self-regulation programs such as codes of ethics certainly bear close scrutiny. Here's how one association thought it was doing good, but didn't have the best results.

The graphic arts market—for posters, prints, and reproductions— had been plagued by pirated versions of original art. Some of the fakes were so good that even experts had trouble distinguishing them from the originals, which of course are far more valuable than the fakes. So a group of art dealers convinced their national association to do something about the problem. A list was created of graphics arts suppliers who were known to have dealt in pirated art. The association published the list and asked members to agree, as a matter of compliance with the association's code of ethics, to not deal with any of the companies on the list. The program was challenged by a "black-listed" art importer; the case ultimately went all the way to the U.S. Supreme Court, which decided that no private association has the right to regulate markets, even to try to exclude firms known to be engaged in illegal conduct.

"I Don't Care What You All Do, I'm Going Ahead"

Meeting discussions that might seem innocuous can have devastating ramifications if they produce anti-competitive results. This story is about association directors who thought they were honoring the law but found out, to their horror, that the opposite was the case.

A local association of recreation vehicle (RV) dealers included on its governing board the owners of all of the larger dealerships in the area. The directors met at dinner once a month to discuss association business, as well as business conditions in the field. At one such meeting a director spoke up to complain about the practice, then common in the area, for dealers to add $100 to the price of each new RV sold to account for "dealer preparation." He noted that his costs were rising rapidly and squeezing the profit he could realize from new RV sales. The director announced that he was immediately going to start charging $200 for dealer preparation on each new RV sale. He said he didn't care what other directors did. Then he promptly left the meeting. In fact, in the coming weeks nearly all of the directors who had attended that dinner meeting raised their dealer preparation charge from the once-standard $100 to $200, which became the new standard in the area. The Department of Justice Antitrust Division obtained criminal indictments against all of those directors who either led the change or followed the leader. Most eventually served time in jail.

What Are the Main Antitrust Risks for You to Know as a Board Member?

Codes of ethics	You should be sure that there are reasonable code standards and fair enforcement procedures, with no ramifications for prices or fees, markets served, or with whom you do business
Standards, testing, and product/service certification	You should be sure that there are reasonable criteria and fair procedures, again with no attempt to limit who can participate in the field
Membership decisions	You should be sure that membership decisions are based exclusively on whether the applicant or existing member meets the objective published criteria for membership; any other considerations could raise scrutiny
Price and fee data	You should be sure that your association follows appropriate guidelines in data surveys and reporting, avoiding lending assistance to any group of users basing anti-competitive decisions on the data
Professional certification	You should be sure that professional certification criteria are reasonable and that due process is afforded all candidates
Discussions at meetings	To the extent that your association can monitor and direct discussions, you should be sure that they do not veer into the dangerous territory of prices or fees, market allocation, or boycotts

Risks from Defamation and Infringement

W ITH THE PROLIFERATION OF communications and information sharing through easy access and negligible expense, an association increasingly serves as the communications hub for the industry, profession, cause, or field of which it represents. With more communication, inevitably there is more risk. As an association director you should be familiar with the rudiments of the principal risks, namely defamation or infringement claims.

Defamation

Associations and their directors frequently communicate within the association or outside of it regarding other people, entities, or products and services. You must take care in all of those communications to avoid defamation. *Defamation* is an oral utterance (*slander*) or written statement (*libel*) made to others (published) of false facts that are damaging to the reputation of an individual, entity, product, or service. You can commit defamation even when you believe you are communicating the truth if instead your statement turns out to be false and damaging. The defamed individual may sue you or anyone who publishes, prints, or repeats the defamation and, depending on the circumstances, may recover money to compensate for the harm to reputation and as punishment as well. In some circumstances, privileges apply that may protect you from legal liability. Most important for this summary, governance discussions within an association are subject to a privilege that protects statements made in those discussions from a claim of defamation; thus, while defaming other directors is not recommended, it bears less legal risk than defaming anyone else outside the context of board deliberations.

In order to help avoid defamation, you should understand the essential elements. First, there must be a particular target of the allegedly offending communication. A statement must be about a particular, living individual or existing entity, or a product or service line. The reference need not be by name; a statement may be defamatory if the listener or reader of the communication understands it to refer to a particular someone or something. Second, a statement must be actually communicated to a third person (in other words, to someone other than the speaker or the subject). Anyone who republishes (i.e., prints, reprints, repeats, paraphrases, or quotes, even with attribution) is equally responsible as the original speaker; therefore an association can be liable for defamation merely by publishing the offending statement of someone else. Third, a statement must be derogatory or damaging to the subject's reputation. Accusing someone of dishonesty or other moral deficiency, or of professional or business deficiency, raises particularly significant risks of liability for defamation. Finally, a statement must be false or misleading. Truth is an absolute defense to virtually any defamation claim, although it can be expensive to engage in litigation to establish the defense. Generally, the allegedly offended party bears the burden of proving that the statement contained a false fact, at least where the statement is about a matter of public concern. In addition, pure opinion utterances (for example, "I loathe that product.") cannot be defamatory; but opinions that reflect false and damaging facts, (for example, "I think that product is defective.") can create defamation liability.

Separate from defamation, another legal risk for you as an association director is *infringement*. Using copyrighted materials or a trademarked name without the permission of the owner is infringing upon the owner's intellectual property. Before going further, you'll want to understand what copyrights and trademarks are, since each is quite different from the other and the two are often confused.

Copyrights and Infringement

Copyright is the ownership one has in what one creates. It is the legal protection afforded an original work set out in some tangible form. It can apply to association newsletters, books, journals, directories, reports, videos, taped educational presentations, website content, etc. Basically, one who creates and sets down an original work also automatically owns it by force of copyright law, absent some other agreement. The owner has the exclusive right to reproduce, adopt, publish, license, or otherwise determine what use is put to that work. For individuals, the protection lasts for the lifetime of the individual plus 70 years (for corporate owners, the term is the earlier of 120 years from creation or 95 years from first publication). The owner also can transfer all of the rights to others or just part of those rights.

There are two important caveats to the basic rule that the creator of original work owns all the rights to that work. First, when someone else pays to have the work created, such as an employer or someone contracting to have the work created, it is the paying party who owns the copyright; this is the *work made for hire doctrine*. The other main nuance is that others have an automatic right to use small portions of an otherwise owned work such as in excerpts for book reviews; they don't have to seek and obtain permission; this is the *fair use exception.* It is sometimes a very complex process to determine how much of a work can be borrowed and for what purposes without infringing upon the copyright owner's rights. Also, there can be significant advantages in obtaining recompense against infringers if one registers one's copyright at the U.S. Copyright Office of the Library of Congress. This can often be accomplished without the aid of an attorney.

For association directors, the main thing here is to avoid assuming that whatever one sees in print or on the web is available for use by the association. This caveat applies to not only written content but also photos, artwork, charts, graphs, music, and videos. Of course important content owned by the association itself should be protected from potential infringers, included via copyright registration where available.

Trademarks and Infringement

A trademark is a name, logo, term, or symbol that the public has come to associate with the provider of goods or services. An association's name, its acronym, and any symbol or logo used by the association, such as for publications, programs, etc., are the most common trademarks of associations. Trademark experts often regard the names of associations as relatively weak marks in that they are often just descriptive (for example, The Widget Association) and not very unique (unlike, for example, Exxon); thus they are sometimes more difficult to have registered or to enforce. Ownership in a trademark is acquired by applying to register with the U.S. Patent and Trademark Office or through commercial use—an association needs to be able to show that its constituency or public has come to relate the trademark to the association or what it provides. Unlike a copyright, the mere conception of a mark, without use or filing with the government, does not generally give rise to any trademark rights. Once the association's trademark has been in use, it is a good practice to seek federal registration for the mark if possible (this permits use of the common registered trademark symbol "®"). Registration is a complex and subtle process which requires the assistance of trademark experts. Registration not only facilitates enforcement of a trademark against infringers but can serve as a scarecrow to ward off others who might try to use your trademark or a confusingly similar mark.

For an association director, obviously the main issue here is avoidance of infringing on the trademarks of others. Care should be taken in choosing an event, program, or other titles or names to avoid using ones that are too similar to those already owned by others. Registration at the U.S. Patent and Trademark Office of the U.S. Department of Commerce should be considered where it is available to protect the association's own intellectual property rights and recognizable identity.

STORIES FROM LIFE

"The Screen and the Fury"

If you thought only people can be defamed, think again; this saga demonstrates how broad the potential victims of defamation can be.

A scientific and engineering society in the field of video reproduction and transmission decides to conduct testing on various kinds of video screens and to publish the results for the benefit of members and others. In one test, John, the expert who evaluated a particular brand of screens, found that the picture reproduced by them seemed to have only muted contrast between the lightest and darkest colors on the screens, which John felt was a real asset in the design and performance of the screens. While incorporating John's comments into the published association report, however, Kathy, the editor, misinterpreted John's comments, assumed they were critical of this brand of screens, and gave the screens very low marks in the report. When the manufacturer of the screens saw the report, it was so offended that it sued the association for defamation. The case went up through three levels of litigation, all the way to the U.S. Supreme

Court, which decided that not only a person or a company, but also a product, can be defamed through the publication of false and damaging information.

"The ABC's of Acronyms"

Trademark infringement can be subtle and nonintuitive. This story demonstrates that an association doesn't always own the rights that its directors might assume it owns.

A professional association embarks on the development and promulgation of a professional certification program to help members' prospective clients identify professionals in this field who have demonstrated that they meet high standards for knowledge and proficiency. Another association in the same field already has a small certification program which has not achieved very strong acceptance by the field; the acronym used in that existing program is ABC. The association which is starting the new program chooses a name for its program which has the acronym CBC—two words of the name, and two letters of the acronym, are identical to those in the other association's existing program. That association sues for trademark infringement. After years of litigation, the infringement suit ultimately fails. The court concludes, on the basis of the plaintiff's evidentiary presentation, that an insufficient case was made that the ABC program's designation has achieved adequate familiarity and acceptance in the field to render a similar designation, CBC, a confusingly similar and infringing one.

What Are the Main Things that Directors Need to Know about Defamation and Infringement?

Defamation	A written or oral statement shared with a third party—whether about an individual, firm, product or service—that is both untrue and damaging; beware of critical pronouncements in association media
Copyright and infringement	The creator's ownership in an original work that is set down in tangible form, not paid for by others (work for hire) nor just a segment for review-type purposes (fair use); beware of borrowing from what others have produced
Trademark and infringement	The ownership right in a name, slogan, logo, etc. that has come to be associated with an association or association program through the association's use of it; beware of using titles too similar to those of others

Risks from Tax Exemption Requirements

A S DISCUSSED EARLIER, ASSOCIATIONS ordinarily enjoy exemption from federal income taxation. That means they do not pay tax on any net surplus that they might achieve from operations each year, i.e., any income in excess of expenses. It is useful for you as an association director to understand some of the basic rules of federal income tax exemption. They affect what your association can and cannot do without risking its tax-exempt status, as well as what activities might result in a federal income tax liability despite the exempt status of the association.

Categories for Tax Exemption

Most associations have exemption under Section 501(c)(6) of the Internal Revenue Code which applies to what the law calls *business leagues*—trade associations, professional societies, and other business or professional organizations. Some have exemption in other categories such as Section 501(c)(3) for charitable, educational, scientific, and religious associations, Section 501(c)(4) for cause-related associations (environmental, seniors, etc.), or Section 501(c)(5) for agricultural associations (this category also applies to labor unions). To qualify for exemption in any of these categories, the association must be organized and operated as a nonprofit and must avoid providing *inurement*—financial advantages to individuals. Furthermore, there are other rules that apply, sometimes to all categories and sometimes to just some of the categories, such as regarding lobbying and political activity, services that benefit only particular individuals or firms rather than the whole field served by the association, or activities that can result in income taxation notwithstanding the association's exemption.

The nonprofit criterion is easy enough to meet, since associations are generally incorporated as nonprofit corporations in their states.

Avoidance of inurement is a more nuanced criterion. At its grossest level, it prohibits exempt associations from paying dividends or making other dividend-like payments to members. Beyond that obvious prohibition, some examples of practices that have been found to violate the inurement ban include: paying legal fees of members; distribution to members of shares of income received from association-owned intellectual property; and rebates to members from the association's net earnings at a trade show. For you as an association director, it's enough to know that inurement is a serious, if elusive, risk to tax exemption. So any proposal before a board from which individual association members may benefit financially should be viewed with some skepticism and evaluated carefully for its tax exemption ramifications.

Unrelated Business Income Tax

Even though an association has been determined to be tax exempt, it is nevertheless subject to taxation on the net return from activities that are not adequately related to the purposes for which the association became tax exempt in the first place. This is called the *unrelated business income tax (UBIT)*. If an association's net revenue that is subject to UBIT becomes substantial in relation to the association's exemption-related revenue, the association is at risk of losing its entire exemption status. The UBIT principle evolved from New York University's acquisition of Mueller's Macaroni Company in the late 1940s. The IRS fought the tax exemption of the arrangement in court and lost. From this decision Congress recognized the need to change the tax exemption law to introduce the UBIT feature.

How does an association, and how do its directors, determine what revenue is subject to UBIT? There are three main criteria: (1) the activity producing the revenue must be a business (usually that means it resembles a commercial undertaking); (2) the business must be carried on regularly (usually that means more frequently than once a year); and—most important—(3) the business must be unrelated (i.e., not "contribute importantly" in the U.S. Supreme Court's words) to the exempt purposes of the association.

For a trade association to operate a restaurant to serve the public is a slam dunk UBIT-eligible activity, for example. There are some activities that Congress, the IRS, or the courts have found to be subject to UBIT. These activities include advertising in association publications (that's the one that attracted the Supreme Court's scrutiny); fee-for-service consulting (associations give a lot of advice and information to members; there may be taxation risks if they charge special fees for customized advice and information);

and redeeming members' customers coupons, bonuses, points, etc. (another actual case).

There are some clear exemptions from UBIT treatment provided by Congress or by the IRS–trade show and exhibition income, selling contributed merchandise, volunteer-managed activities, etc. Perhaps most important is the exemption for passive income—rents, royalties, dividends, and interest. Many associations have *affinity programs* in which they endorse commercial products or services and in return receive exempt royalty income; the key to success in avoiding UBIT taxation in this arrangement is for the associations to keep hands off and leave it mostly to the commercial firms whose products or services are endorsed to market and administer the programs.

What happens if a tax-exempt association has significant UBIT-eligible revenue? Federal income tax is due at corporate rates on the gross revenue from all UBIT-eligible programs less all attributable costs; and a special tax return, the Form 990, is due annually. As noted, if UBIT-eligible revenue becomes substantial compared with exemption-related revenue (dues, registrations, etc.), then the association's entire exemption status is at risk. There is no clear cut-off point when this occurs; one ought to begin worrying when UBIT-eligible revenue reaches 15 to 25 percent of all revenue. Most associations avoid that risk, when they have programs yielding significant UBIT-eligible revenue, by transferring those programs to a controlled for-profit taxable subsidiary; that entity, of course, can have unlimited taxable revenue without endangering the parent association's exemption.

Foundations

Many associations that are not themselves categorized as Section 501(c)(3) charitable, educational, or scientific organizations for tax-exemption purposes have established affiliated and controlled organizations that enjoy the benefits of that exemption category. These foundations may have a range of permissible activities different from those of the main membership associations (and the foundations typically do not have members of their own). Donations to the foundations qualify for charitable tax deductibility for the donors—which is a major incentive in attracting donations, of course. Some government grant opportunities, and many private foundation grant opportunities, may be available only to these foundations. There are some special rules applicable to these foundations, however, that directors should know. For example, there is a very detailed prohibition against such a foundation providing above-market-rate payments to any individual who is in a position to influence decision making by the foundation (called the excess benefit or intermediate sanctions rules). The foundation has a limitation on the extent to which it can engage in lobbying, as well as an absolute prohibition against engaging in any form of political campaign activity. In addition, because donors to a Section 501(c)(3) organization can claim charitable deductibility for their donations, there are strict limits on how that organization can use its assets. For example, a Section 501(c)(6) association can choose to use some of its assets to support a related Section 501(c)(3) organization; but the reverse is often not true.

Foundations affiliated with associations have some distinct advantages and opportunities; but they also carry some special risks in return.

Information Return

Each tax-exempt association, other than a very small one and some special types, must file an annual information return that was promulgated by the IRS just for use by exempt entities; it is called the Form 990. In addition to requiring detailed disclosure of the association's annual financial performance, this tax return also attempts to promote good governance by exempt organizations. It asks more than a dozen questions about governance of these exempt organizations. The IRS has stated that, by asking these questions, it hopes to induce exempt organizations to adopt good governance practices. The form requires a "yes" or "no" answer to each governance question. For example, it asks whether the association maintains governance policies that have IRS-stipulated characteristics on: (1) conflicts of interest, (2) whistleblower protection, (3) document retention/destruction, (4) executive compensation, and (5) joint ventures with businesses. Elsewhere the form asks if the association has shared the draft Form 990 with directors prior to it being filed.

An association director should be aware that, once filed, the association must make the Form 990s available to any member of the public who asks to see them. Thus, unlike personal or business corporation tax returns, the Form 990s are really public documents.

Another thing that is important for a director to know is that the financial disclosures required on the Form 990 are different, and in different formats, from those required by accounting rules for financial audit reporting. Often the numbers in the two different documents cannot be easily reconciled; so a director should not automatically assume that one set of disclosures, whether on the Form 990 or the audited financial report, is necessarily better or more accurate. Usually they are just different.

"Founding Members"

To what extent can financial privileges be afforded to members who were instrumental in conceiving, capitalizing, and otherwise bringing into existence and success a tax-exempt association? Directors might be surprised to learn that such privileges are very limited, as this incident shows.

A group of talented and distinguished professionals in the arts came together to form a national professional association. Many contributed significant time and money to get the association off the ground and even for the first few years while it was in a nascent state. Ultimately the association achieved considerable financial success, owing especially to an annual exhibition of members' work that the association developed and sponsored. To help reward those association members who were there at the beginning, a "Founding Member" category was created. Each founding member was accorded a variety of special privileges. In particular, each one who participated in the annual exhibition received a share of the profits that the association realized at the exhibition. The IRS audited the association and learned of the profit distribution to founding members. It revoked the entire tax-exempt status of the association and assessed back taxes due, interest on the back taxes, and additional penalties, all for a several-year period. The association fought the revocation in court, but ultimately lost.

"An Affinity for Trouble"

Many associations have found that there's a glass ceiling that effectively limits dues income; so they look for ways to build association revenues through nondues sources. Affinity programs can be particularly fruitful. But one must tread carefully, as this story illustrates.

Ken is a newly elected director of a large trade association in the energy industry. Ken's company has struggled for years to maintain liability insurance that has both broad coverage and affordable premiums. In chatting with fellow association directors, he learns that this is a common problem in the industry. Ken approaches his insurance agency contact Beth for possible solutions. Beth proposes to the association a group affinity insurance program in which members can purchase an insurance policy customized for the industry and enjoy favorable premiums due to association-promulgated loss control standards, certification, and education endeavors. In return for sponsoring the program, the association will receive several percentage points of all of the insurance premiums paid into the program by members, a considerable financial windfall for the association. The association's board considers and adopts Beth's proposal. It requires the association to not only make members aware of the new sponsored affinity insurance program, but also to aggressively market the program to members such as through periodic newsletters, direct mail, and internet advertising; a booth at the annual trade show manned by association staff; and direct solicitation at association educational events. The program's premium base builds quickly; and the association begins enjoying six-figure nondues revenue from it. But along comes an IRS audit of the association and the affinity program. IRS finds that the association has not remained sufficiently passive in regard to the program, and asserts that all of the association's revenue from the program is tainted by its aggressive marketing efforts. The association is required to pay back taxes, interest, and penalties.

What Do Association Directors Need to Remember about Tax Exemption?

Categories	Section 501(c)(3)—charitable, educational, scientific, religious Section 501(c)(4)—cause-related Section 501(c)(5)—agricultural (and labor unions) Section 501(c)(6)—business and professional
Main requirements	Organized as a nonprofit; no special advantages to individuals (inurement)
Unrelated Business Income Tax (UBIT)	Taxes are assessed on the net return from a business activity, that is regularly carried-on, and that is not substantially related to the purposes for which tax exemption was granted

Risks from Lobbying and Political Activity

AN ASSOCIATION OFTEN EXISTS to provide one voice for its industry, profession, cause, or field in local, state, or federal public policy matters. An association's directors are often the key actual voices who articulate the association's positions. Thus you should be aware of the laws and regulations that pertain to lobbying, as well as to the supporting function of political activity. For simplicity, this text addresses federal-level lobbying and political activity; state and local jurisdictions may have parallel, but different, regulation schemes. It is important to note that associations with Section 501(c)(3) tax exemption are limited in the extent of lobbying they can conduct and are absolutely prohibited from any political activity.

Lobbying Disclosure

Federal law regarding lobbying essentially requires initial registration and periodic reporting of lobbying contacts and activities. These include communications and background endeavors related to legislation and regulation. They also include efforts to influence the administration of a federal program or policy (including federal contracts and grants). The more general function, typical of much association public policy work, involving education or briefing of legislative or administration officials about the association's field, is not considered lobbying if it does not involve advocating legislative or administrative changes. The law requires an association which conducts lobbying to register with both houses of Congress. An association itself registers for any in-house lobbyists that it employs; a key consideration is that an association employee who spends less than 20 percent of working time on lobbying is not considered a lobbyist. An outside lobbying firm registers for each lobbying client that engages the firm (thus relieving the client of that obligation if the client does no more than very modest amounts of lobbying in-house). Associations and outside lobbying firms that register also must file periodic reports about their lobbying activities that describe which matters are the subjects of their lobbying and disclose how much money is spent on the lobbying. There are special reports required of lobbyists on payments or gifts and on campaign contribution bundling.

Compliance with the law requires an understanding of its subtleties; this is not something that is prudent for non-experts to attempt. Noncompliance can result in serious criminal and civil penalties. Accordingly, associations that engage in any federal-level lobbying should pay careful attention to the law and comply scrupulously with its requirements.

Dues Nondeductibility

Lobbying expenses cannot be deducted for federal income tax purposes. A corollary is that dues paid to associations that engage in lobbying are also nondeductible to the extent that the associations incur lobbying expenses. This rule mostly affects Section 501(c)(6) tax-exempt organizations—trade associations, professional societies, and other business groups. The association must estimate its dues income and federal or state lobbying expenses in advance for the coming year and, on the basis of the difference between those two estimates, must notify the association members what percentage of their dues for that year will not be tax deductible by the members. Alternatively the association can pay a flat 35 percent excise tax on the lobbying expenses it has incurred in the previous year.

Political Activity

There is a century-old federal law prohibiting corporations, including incorporated associations, from using their corporate funds to make political contributions to federal candidates. Some states do permit corporate campaign contributions to state candidates. A now-famous 2010 U.S. Supreme Court decision, *Citizens United,* permits the use of corporate funds to make *independent expenditures*—payments to advance a candidacy but not coordinated with the candidate or candidate's campaign committee.

Beyond that, the main way for an association to engage in political activity is by establishing and administering a political action committee (PAC) to consolidate and direct members' individual campaign contributions to candidates sympathetic to the association's views. While the association usually cannot expend its own funds as campaign contributions, it is indeed permitted to use its own funds for the administrative expenses of the PAC. You might be asked as an association director to make contributions to the association's affiliated PAC or to solicit contributions from others to the PAC. There are statutory limits on the amounts that individuals can contribute to PACs. Also, there are extensive regulations administered by the Federal Election Committee (FEC) for PAC governance, solicitation of contributions, expenditures to candidates, recordkeeping, and periodic reporting to the FEC. A particularly noteworthy provision is that an association cannot solicit a PAC contribution from the executive of a corporate member without first obtaining permission from the corporate member to make that solicitation.

As with lobbying regulation, there are serious criminal and civil penalties for violations in the political activity area (and, again, all political activity is banned for Section 501(c)(3) tax-exempt organizations); strict compliance is essential.

Gifts and Honoraria

It is of course a serious crime to attempt to bribe a government official—where something of value is provided as a *quid pro quo* for favorable government treatment. But even where there is no *quid pro quo* element, there are laws at the federal level that limit gifts and honoraria to members of Congress and their staffs as well as to executive branch officials. Special and more rigorous Congressional limits apply to gifts from registered lobbyists, foreign principals, or private entities that retain or employ such individuals. There are slightly different rules for the U.S. Senate and the U.S. House of Representatives. The laws prohibit staff, officials and members of Congress from accepting certain gifts or honoraria; and they prohibit others from making them. Usually things of very nominal value, such as food and refreshments that are not part of a meal or baseball hats and T-shirts, are exempted. In the Congressional rules there is a long list of qualified exceptions. The Executive Branch rules prohibit gifts, unless an exception applies. Appointees of the Obama Administration are subject to even much stricter restrictions under an Executive Order on Ethics. As with lobbying and political activity, the laws are complex and nonintuitive; it is easy to violate them inadvertently. You as an association director might well be cast in the role of the presenter of these gifts or honoraria. So, once again, careful compliance with the help of experts is warranted.

"The Edge of Schmooze"

There is sometimes a fine line between chatting up a legislator and lobbying that legislator; this story exposes where the grey area becomes black and white.

Jill is an elected director of a national health care professionals' association which has full-time government relations specialists on staff. Jill accepts an invitation to come to Washington, DC, with the association covering her expenses, for the association's annual two-day "fly-in" on federal legislative issues. Unfortunately her schedule does not permit her to attend the first day's session During that session other attendees are briefed on key issues for the association and on which issues that they should address with members of Congress whom they will be meeting the next day. On the second day Jill joins a delegation from the association, including one of its government relations staffers, in meeting a key Congressman who chairs a committee with health care jurisdiction; Jill is acquainted with the Congressman. The other attendees limit their remarks to explaining what the professionals do in this field, what are their main concerns as professionals, and how current laws and regulations impact their profession. The Congressman mentions a bill pending before his committee, summarizes what the bill tries to do, and asks if the association can support the bill. Jill blurts out, "I think one of our association's research studies addresses how great that result would be for our profession; so I think we definitely would favor its enactment. However, we probably would have a few tweaks to the language of the bill such as lowering its triggering threshold." Jill's remarks, whether planned or not, have likely converted a non-lobbying meeting into a lobbying meeting. The association will need to identify this issue in its periodic public reports, and disclose fairly apportioned shares of all of the related expenses of the "fly-in," including for association staff time, for attendees' travel expense reimbursement, and even for the earlier research study.

"Room with a View"

The laws regulating political campaign expenditures have a broad reach. Sometimes a situation that does not even seem to involve politics, or campaigning, or expenditures turns out to involve all three concurrently, as this story shows.

Jack is a prominent businessman from Texas. In his personal capacity he has often made contributions to the campaigns of the state's two-term senior U.S. Senator. Jack has even helped organize fundraisers for the Senator, whom he counts as a friend and who has "thrown his hat in the ring" by announcing an intention to serve a third term in the Senate if re-elected. Jack sits on the board of his national trade association, headquartered in Washington, DC, with a board room overlooking the U.S. Capitol. The association engages in no lobbying and has no PAC; it leaves those functions to another larger trade association in the field. Jack suggests to the association CEO that he could likely score the attendance of his friend, the Senator, at a strictly "meet and greet" "non-political" reception following the association's next board meeting in Washington, DC. The reception turns out to be a gala event; Jack introduces his friend the Senator, noting only in passing that the Senator is seeking re-election. The Senator's staffer has left campaign donation forms at the doors to the board room. A few months later the association finds itself under investigation by the U.S. Department of Justice on behalf of the Federal Election Commission for making illegal in-kind political campaign contributions to the Senator's campaign—the value of the board room rental, the catering expenses, the staff time, invitations, and other costs related to the event. The association ultimately settles by paying a large fine and has its name splashed throughout the newspaper headlines.

What Are Key Issues for Directors on Federal Lobbying and Political Activity?

Lobbying disclosure	Associations that have representatives who engage in lobbying contacts and activities trigger lobbying registration and reporting obligations, whether by the associations themselves, by their engaged lobbying firms, or by both
Political campaign expenditures	Using association funds to make political campaign contributions for federal candidates, other than indirect expenditures, is prohibited
Political Action Committees (PACs)	There are detailed rules governing the formation and operation of an affiliated political action committee (PAC) to channel members' contributions to federal candidates
Gifts and honoraria	Both houses of Congress and the federal agencies limit the nature and value of gifts or honoraria that may be given to government officials

How Can You Minimize the Legal Risks?

T SHOULD BE APPARENT by now that there are many legal pitfalls for associations and their directors. How do you avoid those pitfalls? A few suggestions are offered here.

Top-Down Commitment to Compliance

First, and perhaps most essential, is a top-down commitment by you and your association directors to operate fully within the law. Where the law is unclear, a conservative approach is warranted. You are justly proud to serve as an association director; you want your term to be totally focused on advancing the association and its cause. You are not interested in accepting any acute risk of becoming embroiled in governmental or private legal disputes, with their attendant diversion from the association's mission, seemingly endless delays, difficult-to-control costs, and potential adverse affects on image.

Education

Education is important. A key element in any legal compliance effort is frequent explanation and updating on the legal risks facing your association. Many legal concepts that arise in the association context, for example apparent authority, UBIT, and fair use, are nonintuitive. Your orientation as a director, and that of each new director, should have a component on unique association law compliance challenges.

The availability to directors of knowledgeable, experienced, and trusted legal counsel is also essential. The association should identify and engage one attorney or a team of attorneys based upon reputation and credentials in assisting other nonprofit organizations. Counsel should be charged with the role of monitoring the association's policies and programs and bringing issues of potential risk to the attention of the directors.

Indemnification

Every state permits nonprofit corporations to indemnify their directors. *Indemnification* can be written into the association's bylaws, or effected merely by a board resolution when necessary. Indemnification is the promise of the association to pay for the legal defense—and any ultimate damages—if you as a director are accused of legal wrongdoing while acting on behalf of the association. Indemnification would not apply, though, if you are found to have been acting in a fraudulent or grossly negligent way.

Insurance

The ultimate safety net—insurance. There are many carriers that offer broad liability insurance policies tailored to the needs of nonprofit organizations including associations. The policies ordinarily treat as insured parties not only the association entity itself but also all volunteers, including directors. Most policies will pay the legal defense costs and any resulting settlements or damages from claims of wrongdoing by the insured association or its leadership, including in the areas in which claims against associations are most frequent and most serious.

Minimizing Legal Risks to an Association Director

Top-down commitment to compliance	Directors must adopt and communicate throughout the association a sense of awareness and avoidance of excessive legal risk
Education	Updating on the areas of risk at board orientation of directors and elsewhere
Indemnification	The association's commitment to cover a director if accused of wrongdoing while working for the association
Insurance	Insurance coverage tailored to the unique risks and needs of nonprofit organizations, such as associations

RESOURCES

Association Law Handbook, Fifth Edition, Jerald A. Jacobs,
   Washington, D.C.: ASAE & The Center for Association Leadership,
   2011.

Certification and Accreditation Law Handbook, Second Edition, Jerald
   A. Jacobs and Jefferson C. Glassie, Washington, D.C.: American
   Society of Association Executives, 2004.

Nonprofit Mergers & Joint Ventures, Jerald A. Jacobs,
   Washington, D.C.: American Society of Association Executives,
   2012.

ABOUT THE AUTHOR

Jerald A. Jacobs is an attorney in Washington, DC who focuses on counseling and advocacy for business, professional, social welfare, philanthropic, and other nonprofit organizations. He serves as General Counsel to ASAE: The Center for Association Leadership, the major national association of nonprofit organization executive leadership, and its research affiliate the ASAE Foundation. He has taught nonprofit organization law at graduate law schools and business schools. He has been recognized by the American Bar Association for his work in the nonprofit organization field. He has advised the governments of the European Union and the People's Republic of China on their laws for associations/nongovernmental organizations.